OUR GREAT STATES

WHAT'S GREAT ABOUT
OKLAHOMA?

✳ Sheri Dillard

LERNER PUBLICATIONS ✳ MINNEAPOLIS

CONTENTS

Copyright © 2015
by Lerner Publishing Group, Inc.

Content Consultant: Sterling Evans, Professor of History, University of Oklahoma

Lerner Publications Company
A division of Lerner Publishing Group, Inc.
241 First Avenue North
Minneapolis, MN 55401 USA

For reading levels and more information, look up this title at www.lernerbooks.com.

Main body text set in ITC Franklin Gothic Std Book Condensed 12/15.
Typeface provided by Adobe Systems.

Library of Congress Cataloging-in-Publication Data

Dillard, Sheri.
   What's great about Oklahoma? / by Sheri Dillard.
      pages cm. — (Our great states)
   Includes index.
   ISBN 978-1-4677-3863-7 (lib. bdg. : alk. paper)
      ISBN 978-1-4677-6265-6 (eBook)
   1. Oklahoma—Juvenile literature.
I. Title.
F694.3.D55 2015
976.6—dc23   2014022190

Manufactured in the United States of America
1 - PC - 12/31/14

OKLAHOMA Welcomes You!

Oklahoma is a state full of adventure! There are many fun ways to explore this great state. Can you hear the drumbeat from an American Indian parade marching by? Come learn a new dance at one of the local American Indian festivals. Celebrate cowboys and the American West at a rodeo. Hear the thundering sound of hundreds of hooves at a roundup. Maybe you'll see a bison herd roaming through the prairie. Read on to discover ten things that make Oklahoma great. Then pack a cowboy hat and some hiking boots and stop by for a visit!

Black Mesa
(4,973 feet/
1,516 m)

KANSAS

MISSOURI

TEXAS

Miles
0 20 40 60
0 40 80
Kilometers

Enid

OZARK
PLATEAU

Arkansas River

Stillwater

Tulsa

Broken Arrow

Canadian River

Oklahoma
City

Edmond

Midwest City

Moore

Norman

ARKANSAS

N

WICHITA
MOUNTAINS

Lawton

ARBUCKLE
MOUNTAINS

OUACHITA
MOUNTAINS

Lake
Texoma

Red River

TEXAS

Explore Oklahoma's
prairies and all the places
in between. Just turn the
page to find out all about
the SOONER STATE. >

RAM NATIONAL CIRCUIT FINALS RODEO

> Round up your friends and family and head over to Guthrie. Guthrie hosts one of the country's biggest rodeos! Cheer on cowboys and cowgirls at the Ram National Circuit Finals Rodeo. They compete here for a national championship. There are several action-packed events to see. Watch riders try to stay on bucking broncos and lasso steer. And don't miss the funny rodeo clown shows. Yeehaw!

While you're in Guthrie for the rodeo, be sure to check out the town. Guthrie was Oklahoma's first capital. There is plenty to do in this old frontier town. Start off with a trolley tour. You'll drive by Oklahoma's oldest saloon and Guthrie's first train depot. Then browse the many shops. Maybe you'll find your own cowboy gear. And if you work up an Oklahoma-sized appetite, grab some grub at one of the many restaurants.

WILL ROGERS

One of Oklahoma's best-known cowboys was Will Rogers. He grew up on a ranch and became good at lassoing steer. His trick-roping skills earned him a spot in the *Guinness World Records*! He used his rope skills in Wild West shows. He also acted on Broadway and in movies. He had a radio show and even wrote for a newspaper.

See the town of Guthrie on the
First Capital Trolley.

OKLAHOMA CITY ZOO
AND BOTANICAL GARDEN

> Come visit one of the oldest zoos in the Southwest! You'll see everything from apes to zebras. Prowl over to the Oklahoma Trails area to see grizzly bears and black bears. Saunter by the Cat Forest to watch snow leopards and jaguars travel through mazelike trails. Don't miss the Children's Zoo section. It has a petting zoo and a splash park. There is plenty of space to run, crawl, and climb. Scale the rope structure like a spider monkey. You can even give nectar to a lorikeet, a small parrot. But be prepared. You may end up with an armful of lorikeets looking for a taste.

Want to visit the Botanical Garden section of the zoo? That's easy! The entire zoo is a garden! Check out the largest outdoor butterfly garden in Oklahoma. Walk among unusual trees such as Chinese parasol trees and alligator junipers. Get ideas for your own garden. Many of the vegetables and herbs in this garden are used to feed the zoo animals.

Pet different animals, including anacondas, at the Oklahoma City Zoo and Botanical Garden!

Buy nectar from the zoo to feed the lorikeets.

ALABASTER CAVERNS
STATE PARK

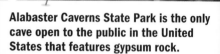

Alabaster Caverns State Park is the only cave open to the public in the United States that features gypsum rock.

> Head underground at the Alabaster Caverns State Park near Freedom. There are two great reasons to visit this park. First, there is a 0.75-mile (1.2-kilometer) cavern open for tours. And it is a true bat cave! Look up as you walk through the cavern. Can you spot bats hanging from the ceiling?

The second great reason to visit the cavern is to see the alabaster cave walls. Alabaster is a rare kind of gypsum rock. As you walk through, admire the white, pink, and black gypsum. The gypsum cave walls sparkle like jewels! When you're done touring the cave, relax at the park's picnic area. Play volleyball or horseshoes. Or just grill some hot dogs for lunch. You can camp at the park overnight if you really don't want to leave!

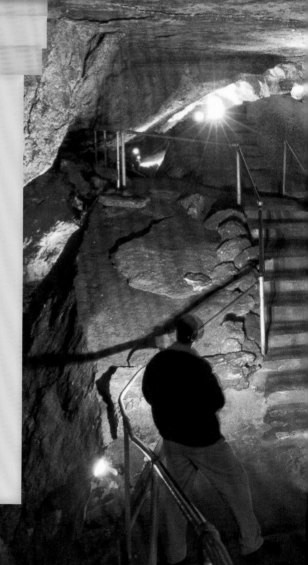

Spot bats hanging from the ceiling inside the Alabaster Caverns.

ROUTE 66

> Route 66 runs all the way from Chicago, Illinois, to Los Angeles, California. It once was the main road connecting the East and the West. Oklahoma claims the longest stretch of this famed highway. It isn't used much anymore. But there are still many fun sights to see!

The Blue Whale is a popular stop. This giant whale structure is in a small pond in Catoosa. It was once a swimming hole. Kids would zoom down the slide, jump off the tail, and check out a hidden area in the whale's head. This Route 66 landmark is still a popular spot for fishing and picnicking. And it's even possible to venture inside the whale! Bring your camera and snap photos inside the whale.

If you're thirsty, make a stop at POPS in Arcadia. POPS has more than six hundred kinds of soda to choose from! How does watermelon or blue raspberry soda sound? Check out the 66-foot-tall (20-meter) POPS soda bottle at night. It lights up the night sky with a colorful show.

The Blue Whale in Catoosa is 80 feet (24 m) long.

DUST BOWL

In the 1930s, the Great Plains region suffered through many years of drought and dust storms. During this time, the Great Plains became known as the Dust Bowl. Many families had to leave their farms and homes and find work in other states. The Panhandle area of Oklahoma was one of the hardest hit. This northwest area of Oklahoma is called the Panhandle because it looks just like the handle of a pan. Route 66 was the main road for Oklahomans as they headed west to escape the Dust Bowl.

13

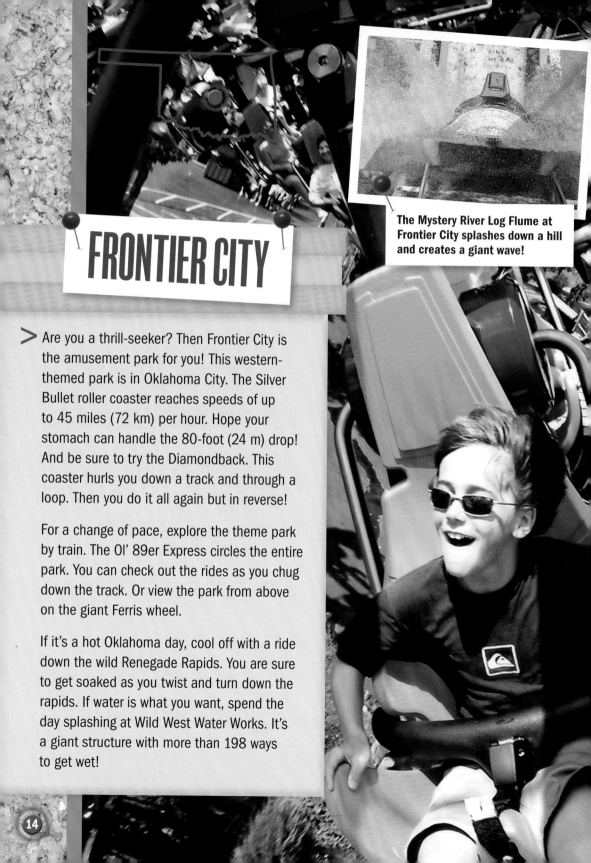

The Mystery River Log Flume at Frontier City splashes down a hill and creates a giant wave!

FRONTIER CITY

> Are you a thrill-seeker? Then Frontier City is the amusement park for you! This western-themed park is in Oklahoma City. The Silver Bullet roller coaster reaches speeds of up to 45 miles (72 km) per hour. Hope your stomach can handle the 80-foot (24 m) drop! And be sure to try the Diamondback. This coaster hurls you down a track and through a loop. Then you do it all again but in reverse!

For a change of pace, explore the theme park by train. The Ol' 89er Express circles the entire park. You can check out the rides as you chug down the track. Or view the park from above on the giant Ferris wheel.

If it's a hot Oklahoma day, cool off with a ride down the wild Renegade Rapids. You are sure to get soaked as you twist and turn down the rapids. If water is what you want, spend the day splashing at Wild West Water Works. It's a giant structure with more than 198 ways to get wet!

Let your feet dangle as you ride Frontier City's Silver Bullet roller coaster.

WICHITA MOUNTAINS WILDLIFE REFUGE

Watch for prairie dogs as you hike through the Wichita Mountains Wildlife Refuge.

> The Wichita Mountains Wildlife Refuge near Lawton has something for everyone. Watch the many kinds of animals that live in the refuge. Or head out on an exciting hike. Be ready to climb, jump, and crawl through this landscape.

There are sixteen different trails to hike. They are all different lengths, so you can choose which one is best for you. Follow the trails through forests, across prairie grasses, and over rocky mountains. Maybe your trail will give you a view of the boulders known as Apple and Pear. These giant boulders are the size of houses! They sit high above the Valley of the Boulders. Or maybe you'll hike to one of the summits. Here, you'll have a beautiful view of the refuge and its animals. You just might spot the bison, elk, deer, prairie dogs, and longhorn cattle that live here.

AMERICAN BISON

The Wichita Mountains Wildlife Refuge was created in 1901 to protect wild animals that were in danger of becoming extinct. Millions of bison roamed the country in the early 1800s. But bison were often hunted for their meat and hide. By 1900, there were only several hundred left. Bison numbers have since risen to more than 250,000. Roughly 650 of them live in the Wichita Mountains Wildlife Refuge.

TURNER FALLS PARK

> One of Oklahoma's greatest summer spots is Turner Falls Park. Cool, clear water flows through the entire park. It is home to natural swimming pools. And you can't miss the 77-foot-tall (23 m) waterfall! It is the largest waterfall in the state. Jump in and enjoy the many natural pools. When you're done hiking and swimming, go horseback riding through the park.

There are many hiking trails around the waterfall. One trail leads to an old stone castle. Even though the castle was abandoned long ago, it is still a fun place to stop for a visit. It's perfect for exploring! Pretend to defend the castle or play a game of hide-and-seek. Don't miss the view from the top of the tower. Camp at the park and enjoy it all again the next day!

Take to the Turner Falls Park trails on horseback.

Turner Falls Park is located in the Arbuckle Mountains.

THE RED EARTH NATIVE AMERICAN CULTURAL FESTIVAL

> Watch the streets of downtown Oklahoma City come alive with color and excitement! The Red Earth Native American Cultural Festival starts off with a parade. Drum groups and dancers all dress in their very finest traditional clothes.

Witness a dance competition. The contestants are some of the best American Indian dancers in the world. You can watch and learn a few dance moves yourself! Cool down with a stroll through the Art Market. Be sure to check out the winners from the youth art contest. There's even an area where you can make your own crafts and jewelry. And don't forget about the food! Sample some tasty American Indian tacos.

More than thirty thousand people attend the Red Earth Native American Cultural Festival each year.

AMERICAN INDIAN HISTORY

American Indians played a large role in Oklahoma's history. In the 1830s, the federal government demanded that American Indians move from the southeastern United States to "Indian Territory." This area is now Oklahoma. They were moved because white settlers wanted American Indian land for farming. If the American Indians didn't leave on their own, the US military forced them out. The trip was more than 1,000 miles (1,600 km). Most people had to walk. Their journey was filled with suffering and sadness. It came to be called the Trail of Tears. Thousands of American Indians died from hunger, exhaustion, and disease.

THE HITCHING POST AT BLACK MESA

> For a true ranch experience, stay a night or two at the Hitching Post at Black Mesa. It is located in the western area of Oklahoma's Panhandle. Ride horses, help drive cattle, and even watch a calf branding. Do you like cowboy tricks? Learn how to rope and test your skill on the ranch's obstacle course.

Experience an original stagecoach ride. The stagecoach was used to carry US mail back in 1882. If you like to fish, find a shady spot by the river. Cook out with your fellow cowboys and cowgirls and sing campfire songs under the starry sky. And don't forget to ask the owners to show you the best place to find dinosaur tracks! Dinosaurs once roamed this area.

Some fossils of dinosaur footprints can be seen near the Hitching Post.

BLACK MESA

Black Mesa is Oklahoma's highest point at 4,973 feet (1,516 m). It is millions of years old. Hardened lava from a volcano formed it. You can see exposed rocks from the time of dinosaurs. Maybe you'll find a dinosaur bone fossil! Black Mesa is also a popular spot for stargazing. If you visit in August, be sure to join the crowds that gather to watch the annual meteor shower!

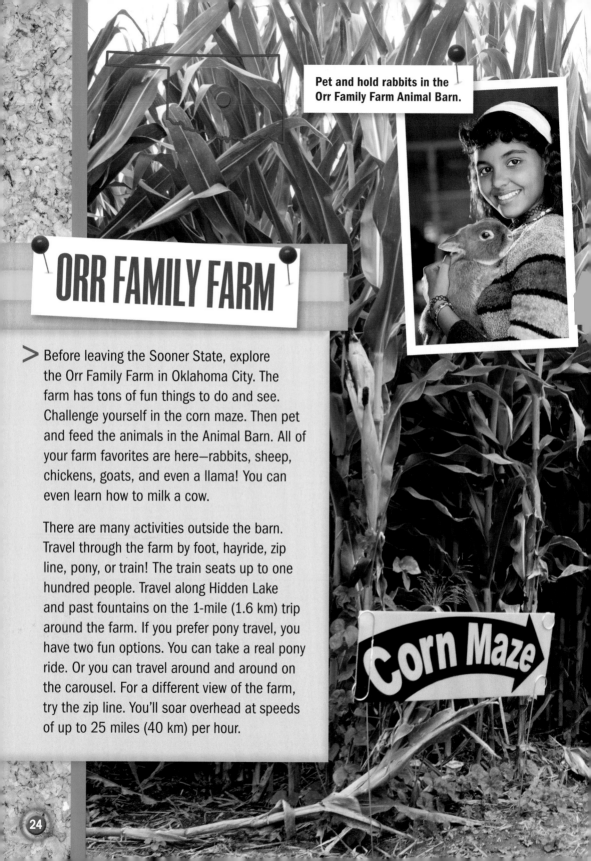

Pet and hold rabbits in the Orr Family Farm Animal Barn.

ORR FAMILY FARM

> Before leaving the Sooner State, explore the Orr Family Farm in Oklahoma City. The farm has tons of fun things to do and see. Challenge yourself in the corn maze. Then pet and feed the animals in the Animal Barn. All of your farm favorites are here—rabbits, sheep, chickens, goats, and even a llama! You can even learn how to milk a cow.

There are many activities outside the barn. Travel through the farm by foot, hayride, zip line, pony, or train! The train seats up to one hundred people. Travel along Hidden Lake and past fountains on the 1-mile (1.6 km) trip around the farm. If you prefer pony travel, you have two fun options. You can take a real pony ride. Or you can travel around and around on the carousel. For a different view of the farm, try the zip line. You'll soar overhead at speeds of up to 25 miles (40 km) per hour.

Corn Maze

You've read about ten awesome things to see and do in Oklahoma. Now think about what your Oklahoma top ten list would include. What would you like to see if you visited the state? Make your top ten list on a separate sheet of paper. If you would like, you can even turn your list into a book. Add drawings or pictures from the Internet or magazines.

Feed goats at the Orr Family Farm.

OKLAHOMA BY MAP

> MAP KEY

⭐ Capital city

◯ City

◯ Point of interest

▲ Highest elevation

-·-· State border

—— Route 66

OKLAHOMA

Visit www.lernerresource.com to learn more about the state flag of Oklahoma.

Black Mesa
(4,973 feet/1,516 m)

The Hitching Post at Black Mesa

TEXAS

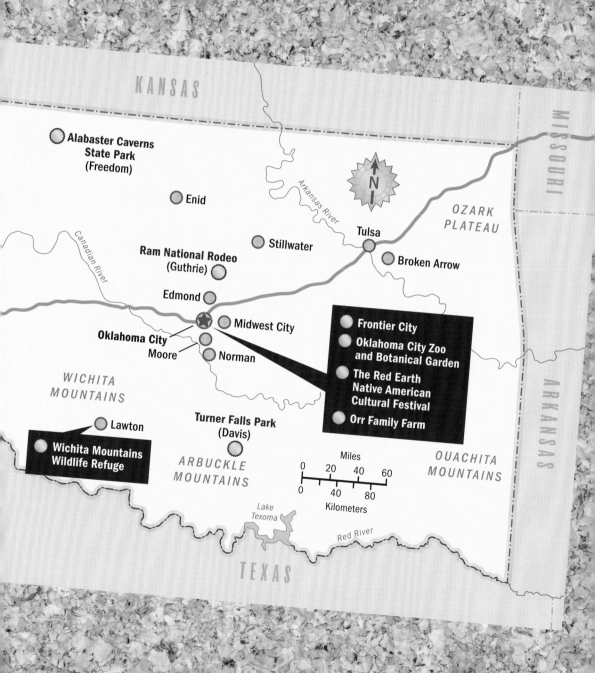

KANSAS

MISSOURI

Alabaster Caverns
State Park
(Freedom)

Enid

Arkansas River

N

OZARK
PLATEAU

Canadian River

Stillwater

Tulsa

Broken Arrow

Ram National Rodeo
(Guthrie)

Edmond

Oklahoma City

Moore

Midwest City

Norman

Frontier City

Oklahoma City Zoo
and Botanical Garden

The Red Earth
Native American
Cultural Festival

Orr Family Farm

ARKANSAS

WICHITA
MOUNTAINS

Lawton

Wichita Mountains
Wildlife Refuge

Turner Falls Park
(Davis)

ARBUCKLE
MOUNTAINS

OUACHITA
MOUNTAINS

Miles
0   20   40   60

0   40   80
Kilometers

Lake
Texoma

Red River

TEXAS

OKLAHOMA FACTS

NICKNAME: The Sooner State

SONG: "Oklahoma" by Richard Rodgers and Oscar Hammerstein II

MOTTO: *Labor Omnia Vincit* (Latin phrase for "Labor Conquers All Things")

FLOWER: Oklahoma rose

TREE: redbud

BIRD: scissor-tailed flycatcher

ANIMAL: American buffalo (bison)

FOODS: strawberries, watermelon

DATE AND RANK OF STATEHOOD: November 16, 1907; the 46th state

CAPITAL: Oklahoma City

AREA: 69,899 square miles (181,038 sq. km)

AVERAGE JANUARY TEMPERATURE: 37°F (3°C)

AVERAGE JULY TEMPERATURE: 82°F (28°C)

POPULATION AND RANK: 3,850,568; 28th (2013)

MAJOR CITIES AND POPULATIONS: Oklahoma City (599,199), Tulsa (393,987), Norman (115,562), Broken Arrow (102,019), Lawton (98,376)

NUMBER OF US CONGRESS MEMBERS: 5 representatives, 2 senators

NUMBER OF ELECTORAL VOTES: 7

NATURAL RESOURCES: fertile soil, trees, oil, natural gas, coal, gypsum, sand, gravel, granite, limestone, clay, salt

AGRICULTURAL PRODUCTS: cotton, peanuts, wheat, dairy products, cattle, hogs, broilers (young chickens)

MANUFACTURED GOODS: machinery, petroleum and coal products, metal products, processed foods, plastic and rubber products

STATE HOLIDAYS AND CELEBRATIONS: Oklahoma Day, Oklahoma State Fair

GLOSSARY

alabaster: a smooth, usually white, and nearly transparent gypsum used for carving

botanical: relating to plants

branding: to burn a mark on the skin of cattle or other animals to identify them

cavern: a cave, often of large or unknown size

drought: a long period of dry weather

fossil: a trace of an animal or plant from millions of years ago that is preserved as rock

frontier: a distant area where few people live

gypsum: a colorless mineral that consists of calcium sulfate occurring in crystals

meteor: a piece of rock or metal from space that forms a streak of light as it burns and speeds toward the earth

nectar: a sweet liquid produced by plants

refuge: a place that provides shelter or protection

stagecoach: a wagon pulled by horses that carries passengers and mail and runs on a schedule between established stops

FURTHER INFORMATION

Hoena, Blake. *Oklahoma: The Sooner State*. Minneapolis: Bellwether Media, 2014. Read more about Oklahoma's geography, landmarks, and wildlife.

Josephson, Judith Pinkerton. *Why Did Cherokees Move West? And Other Questions about the Trail of Tears.* Minneapolis: Lerner Publications, 2011. Learn more about the long journey that came to be known as the Trail of Tears.

Oklavision
http://www.oklavision.tv
Watch videos and see beautiful pictures of Oklahoma's landscapes and wildlife.

Orr, Tamra. *Oklahoma*. New York: Children's Press, 2014. Read more about Oklahoma's geography, history, and people.

Travel Oklahoma
http://www.travelok.com
Check out this site for even more fun places to visit in Oklahoma.

Welcome to Oklahoma
http://www.ok.gov/portal/view_photo_gallery.php
View more photos of Oklahoma's many landmarks.

INDEX

PHOTO ACKNOWLEDGMENTS

The images in this book are used with the permission of: © John A Davis/Shutterstock Images, pp. 1, 22–23; NASA, pp. 2–3; © Jay Boucher/Shutterstock Images, p. 4; © Shutters⬤ Images, pp. 4–5, 8–9, 25; © Laura Westlund/ Independent Picture Service, pp. 5 (top), 26–27; Library of Congress, p. 6 (LC-USZ62-20553); © Crebbin/Shutterstock Images, pp. 6–7; Serge M⬤ p. 7; © Sue Ogrocki/AP/Corbis, p. 9 (top); © Aleksandar Todorovic/Shutterstock Images, p (bottom); © Bambuh/Shutterstock Images, p. 1⬤ © John Elk III/Alamy, pp. 10–11; © Zeljko Radoj⬤ Shutterstock Images, p. 11; Carol M. Highsmith Archive/Library of Congress, pp. 12–13 (LC-DIG-highsm-04404), 13 (top) (LC-DIG-highsm-0400⬤ National Oceanic and Atmospheric Administratio⬤ p. 13 (bottom); © The Oklahoman, Chris Landsberger/AP Images, pp. 14–15; © Shaun Wilkinson/Shutterstock Images, p. 14; © Natalie419, p. 15; © Scott Payne/Shutterstoc⬤ Images, p. 16; © Deniz Tokatli/Thinkstock, pp. 16–17; © Olivier Le Queinec/Shutterstock Images, p. 17; © Sedin/Shutterstock Images, p. United States Geological Survey, pp. 18–19; © Betty LaRue/Alamy, p. 19; © Jon Arnold Imag⬤ Ltd/Alamy, p. 20; © AP Images, pp. 20–21; © National Geographic Image Collection/Alamy, p. 21; © Tom Bean/Alamy, p. 22; Chris M. Morris⬤ p. 23; © Susan Law Cain/Shutterstock Images, pp. 24–25; © Thinkstock, p. 24; © nicoolay/ iStockphoto, p. 26; © SF photo/Shutterstock Images, p. 29 (top right); US Fish and Wildlife Service, p. 29 (top left); © Denis Larkin/ Shutterstock Images, p. 29 (bottom right); © Va⬤ Lawless/Shutterstock Images, p. 29 (bottom left⬤

Cover: © Justin A. Morris/Moment Open/Getty Images (Wichita Mountains Wildlife Refuge); © iStockphoto.com/Chris Pritchard (Oklahoma City); © Stock Connection/SuperStock (Red Ear⬤ Festival); Carol M. Highsmith/Library of Congress LC-DIG-highsm-04496 (POPS Restaurant); © La⬤ Westlund/Independent Picture Service (map); © iStockphoto.com/fpm (seal); © iStockphoto. com/vicm (pushpins); © iStockphoto.com/benz1⬤ (corkboard).